Learn To Draw
Figure Drawing With Pencil
Step by Step

Figure Drawing Books For Absolute Beginners

By Gala Publication

PUBLISHED BY:

Gala Publication

ISBN-13: 978- 1508673583
ISBN-10: 1508673586

Table Of Content :

Steampunk-Girl

Step1

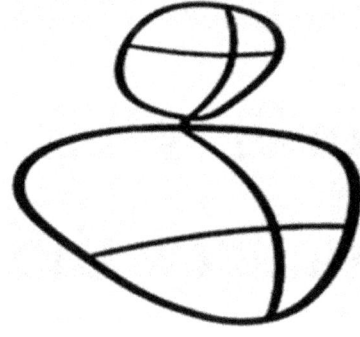

Step2

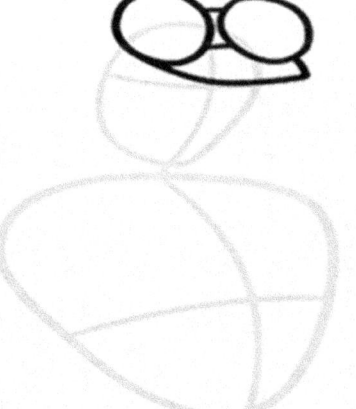

Step3

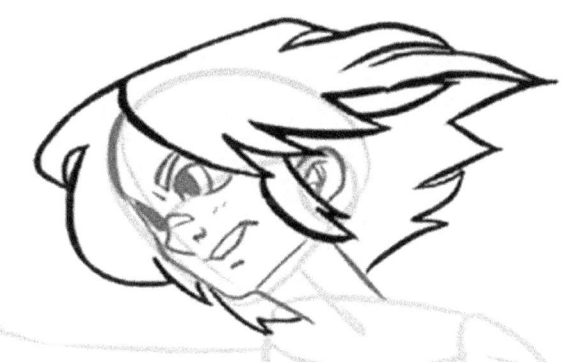

Step4

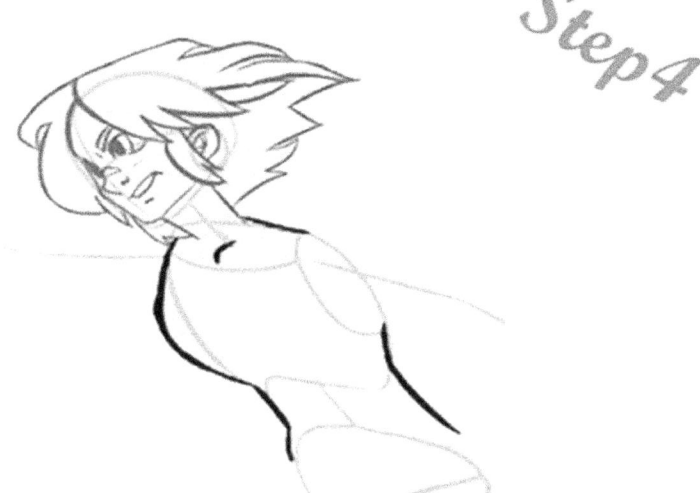

Step5

Step6

Step7

Step8

Princesses

Step1

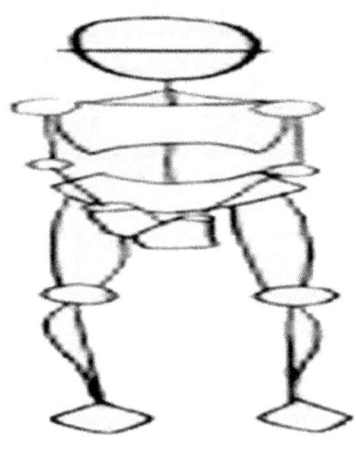

Step2

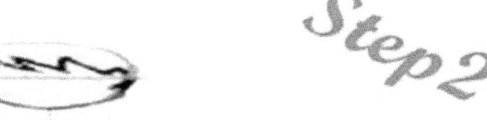

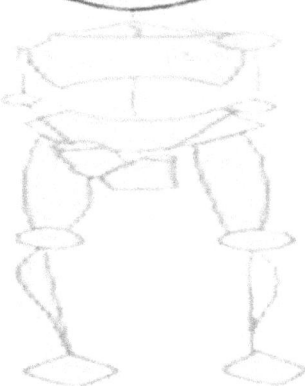

Step3

Step4

Step5

Step6

Step7

Step8

Girl-Crying

Step1

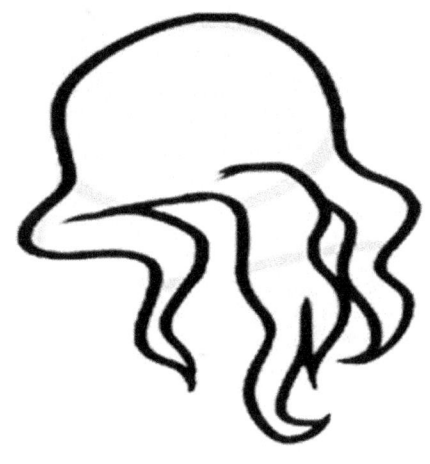

Step2

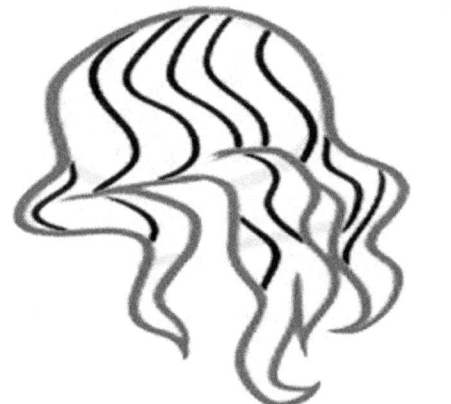

Step3

Step4

Step5

Step6

Surfer-Dude

Step1

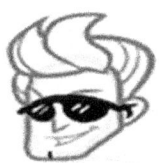

Step2

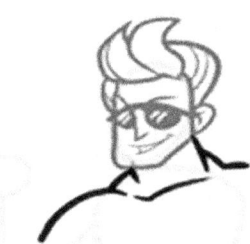

Step3

Step4

Step5

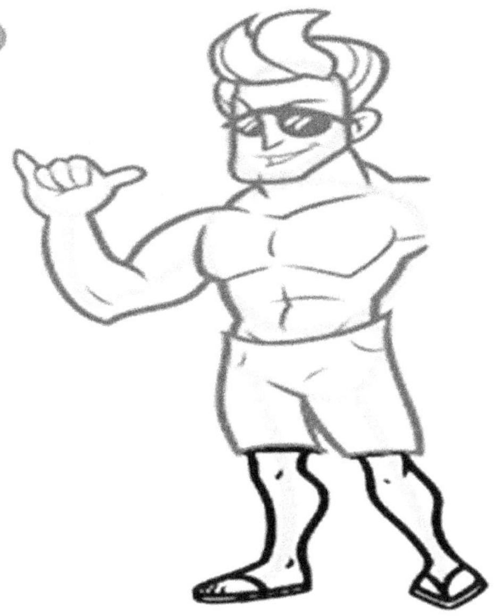

Step6

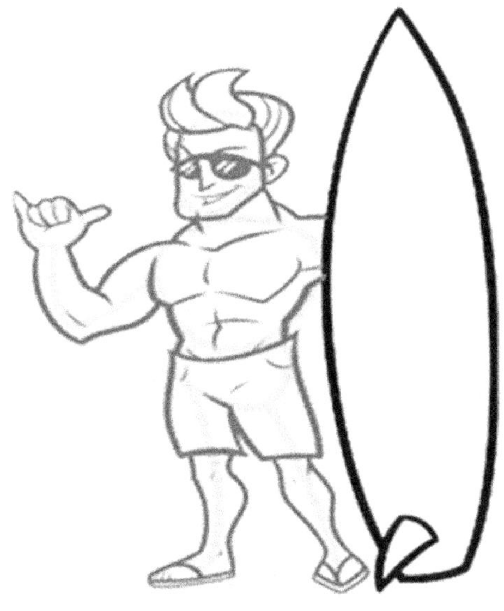

Step7

Step8

Little-Girls

Step1

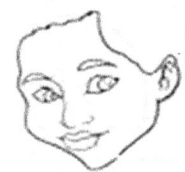

Step2

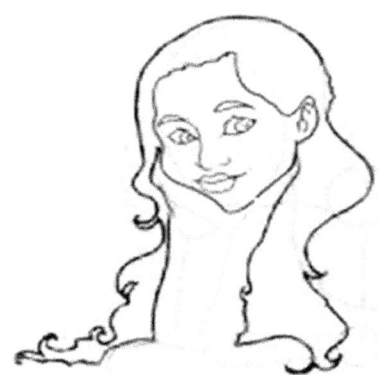

Step3

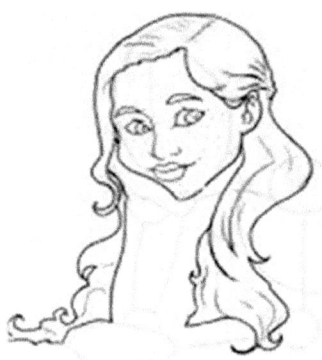

Step4

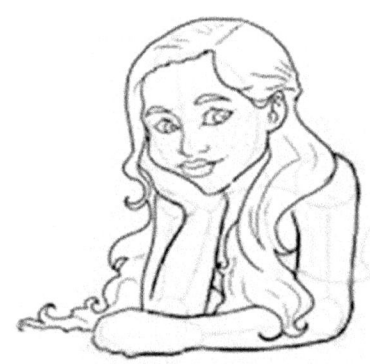

Step5

Step6

Step7

Step8

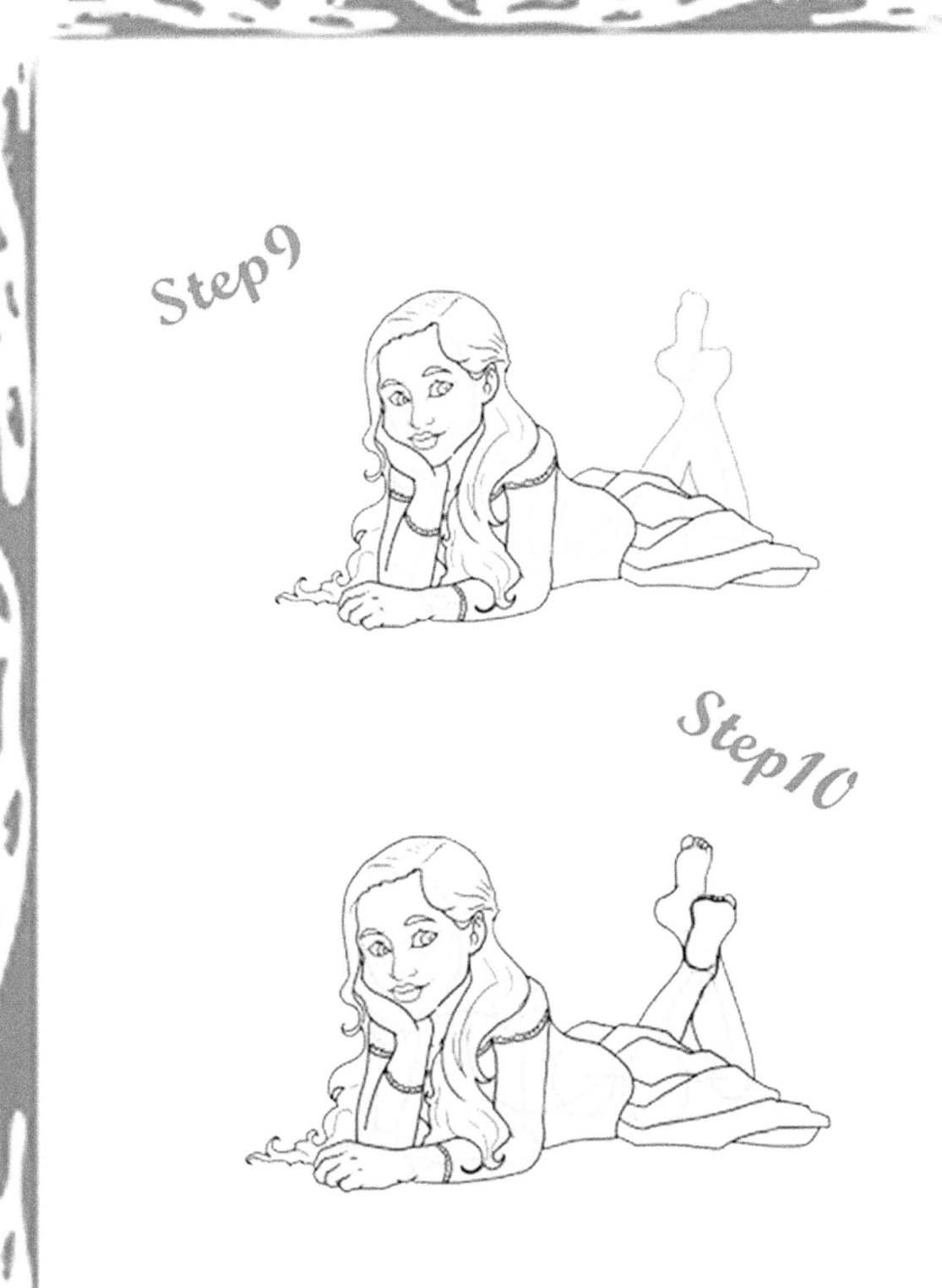

Step9

Step10

THE END